A Note from
Mary Pope Osborne About the

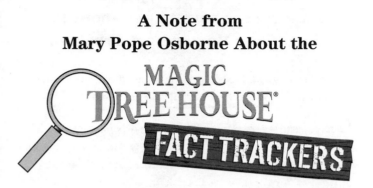

When I write Magic Tree House® adventures, I love including facts about the times and places Jack and Annie visit. But when readers finish these adventures, I want them to learn even more. So that's why we write a series of nonfiction books that are companions to the fiction titles in the Magic Tree House® series. We call these books Fact Trackers because we love to track the facts! Whether we're researching dinosaurs, pyramids, Pilgrims, sea monsters, or cobras, we're always amazed at how wondrous and surprising the real world is. We want you to experience the same wonder we do—so get out your pencils and notebooks and hit the trail with us. You can be a Magic Tree House® Fact Tracker, too!

Mary Pope Osborne

Here's what kids, parents, and teachers have to say about the Magic Tree House® Fact Trackers:

"They are so good. I can't wait for the next one. All I can say for now is prepare to be amazed!" —Alexander N.

"I have read every Magic Tree House book there is. The [Fact Trackers] are a thrilling way to get more information about the special events in the story." —John R.

"These are fascinating nonfiction books that enhance the magical time-traveling adventures of Jack and Annie. I love these books, especially *American Revolution.* I was learning so much, and I didn't even know it!" —Tori Beth S.

"[They] are an excellent 'behind-the-scenes' look at what the [Magic Tree House fiction] has started in your imagination! You can't buy one without the other; they are such a complement to one another." —Erika N., mom

"Magic Tree House [Fact Trackers] took my children on a journey from Frog Creek, Pennsylvania, to so many significant historical events! The detailed manuals are a remarkable addition to the classic fiction Magic Tree House books we adore!" —Jenny S., mom

"[They] are very useful tools in my classroom, as they allow for students to be part of the planning process. Together, we find facts in the [Fact Trackers] to extend the learning introduced in the fictional companions. Researching and planning classroom activities, such as our class Olympics based on facts found in *Ancient Greece and the Olympics,* help create a genuine love for learning!" —Paula H., teacher

MAGIC TREE HOUSE® FACT TRACKER

Twisters
and Other Terrible Storms

A NONFICTION COMPANION TO MAGIC TREE HOUSE #23:
Twister on Tuesday

BY WILL OSBORNE
AND MARY POPE OSBORNE

ILLUSTRATED BY SAL MURDOCCA

A STEPPING STONE BOOK™
Random House 🏠 New York

The Magic Tree House Fact Tracker series was formerly known as the
Magic Tree House Research Guide series.

Visit us on the Web!
SteppingStonesBooks.com
randomhousekids.com

Educators and librarians, for a variety of teaching tools, visit us at
RHTeachersLibrarians.com

Library of Congress Cataloging-in-Publication Data
Osborne, Will.
Twisters and other terrible storms : a nonfiction companion to Magic tree house #23,
Twister on Tuesday / by Will Osborne and Mary Pope Osborne ;
illustrated by Sal Murdocca.
p. cm. — (Magic tree house fact tracker)
"A stepping stone book." Previously published in 2003. Includes index.
ISBN 978-0-375-81358-0 (trade) — ISBN 978-0-375-91358-7 (lib. bdg.) —
ISBN 978-0-307-97526-3 (ebook)
1. Severe storms—Juvenile literature. I. Osborne, Mary Pope.
II. Murdocca, Sal, ill. III. Title.
QC941.3.O78 2011   551.55—dc22   2011010462

Printed in the United States of America
39 38 37

This book has been officially leveled by using the F&P Text Level Gradient™
Leveling System.

For Bill Pope

Scientific Consultant:

ROBERT C. LEVY, Scientist, SSAI, Laboratory for Atmospheres, NASA Goddard Space Flight Center

Education Consultant:

MELINDA MURPHY, Media Specialist, Reed Elementary School, Cypress Fairbanks Independent School District, Houston, Texas

We also thank Paul Coughlin for his ongoing photographic contribution to the series and, as always, our wonderful, creative team at Random House: Joanne Yates, Helena Winston, Diane Landolf, Cathy Goldsmith, Mallory Loehr, and, of course and especially, our wonderful editor, Shana Corey.

TWISTERS
and Other Terrible Storms

Contents

Dear Readers,

The tornado we saw in <u>Twister on Tuesday</u> was really scary! But when it was over, we weren't scared—we were curious! We wondered what causes twisters, and how twisters are different from hurricanes and other storms. We also wondered how weather can change so much from day to day.

When we got back to Frog Creek, we wanted to find the answers to these questions. We decided to track down the facts! We went to the library and checked out books about storms. We watched videos about tornadoes and hurricanes. Our parents

took us to a science museum, where we learned about weather all around the world. Most interesting of all, we started keeping a record of weather changes in our own backyard!

Now we want to share the facts with you.

So get your notebook, get your backpack, and get ready to be blown away by the facts about twisters and other terrible storms.

Jack

Annie

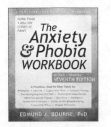

1

Weather

In May, a twister tears through Texas. It picks up whole houses and smashes them to the ground.

In August, a hurricane rages for three days in Florida. It destroys entire towns. Thousands of families lose their homes.

In December, a blizzard covers most of Michigan in deep snow. Icy winds rip roofs off buildings. People are trapped in their homes for days.

These terrible storms seem like nature gone wild. But they're really just a natural part of our Earth's weather.

What *is* weather? Why does the weather change from day to day? Why does it sometimes cause so much damage?

To understand weather, you first have to know about Earth and its *atmosphere* (AT-mus-feer).

The Atmosphere

Our Earth is covered by a blanket of air. This blanket of air is called the atmosphere. The atmosphere makes it possible for humans, animals, and plants to live on Earth.

The air in the atmosphere is made up of different kinds of gases. Two of these gases are *oxygen* and *carbon dioxide*. Humans and animals need the oxygen in the atmosphere to breathe. Plants need

A <u>gas</u> is something that is neither solid nor liquid.

the carbon dioxide in the atmosphere to make food and grow.

The atmosphere also helps control Earth's temperature. During the day, the atmosphere blocks some of the sun's rays so Earth doesn't get too hot. At night, it holds some of the sun's heat so Earth doesn't get too cold.

The Atmosphere
Covers all of Earth
Made of gases
Controls Earth's temperature

The atmosphere is like an ocean of air flowing all around Earth. It is constantly moving and changing. When we talk about weather, we're talking about changes in the part of the atmosphere that's closest to Earth's surface.

Meteorologists

Scientists who study the weather are called *meteorologists* (mee-tee-ur-AHL-uh-jists). *Meteorologist* comes from a Greek word that means "happening in the sky."

Meteorologists use many tools to gather information about the weather. The information helps them predict what the weather might be like in the future.

To **predict** means to tell what will happen in the future.

To become a meteorologist, you need to study science, math, and computers. But the most important thing is to be really interested in the weather!

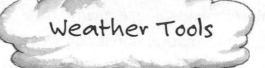

Weather Tools

Many people study weather in their own homes and classrooms.

Here are some common tools for weather watching:

Anemometer
(an-uh-MOM-uh-tur)—
measures wind speed

Wind vane—shows
direction of wind

Wind

Rain gauge (gayge)—
measures rainfall

20

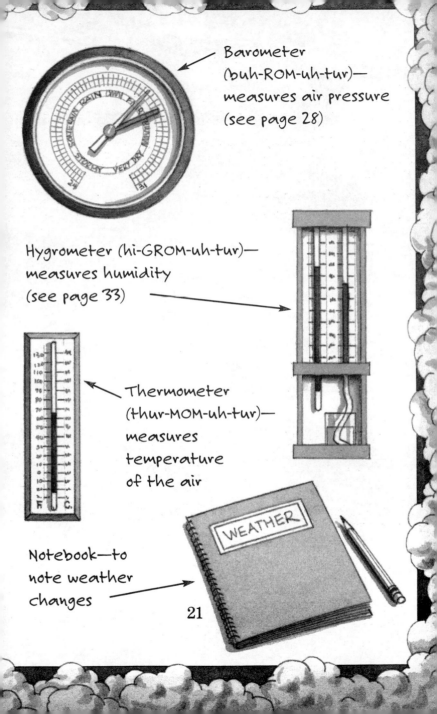

Barometer
(buh-ROM-uh-tur)—
measures air pressure
(see page 28)

Hygrometer (hi-GROM-uh-tur)—
measures humidity
(see page 33)

Thermometer
(thur-MOM-uh-tur)—
measures
temperature
of the air

WEATHER

Notebook—to
note weather
changes

21

2
Wind

Wind is invisible but powerful. It can send sailboats racing across lakes and oceans. It can cool you off on a hot day. It can also destroy whole towns in just a few hours.

Ancient people wondered what caused the wind. The ancient Greeks thought winds were controlled by a god named Aeolus (EE-uh-lus). Aeolus kept the winds in a cave with eight doors. When he wanted a wind to blow, he rolled a rock away from one of the doors.

Aeolus

Today we know that wind is really caused by the uneven heating of the atmosphere.

The Sun

The sun does not warm Earth evenly. On any given day, some places get much hotter than others.

Warm air is lighter than cold air. So when an area of Earth's surface is warmed by the sun, the air above that area rises up toward the sky.

Whenever warm air rises, air from another spot moves in to take its place. We call the moving air *wind*.

Weather changes because of all the warm air and cool air moving around. If there were no wind, the weather would never change!

The sun doesn't actually heat air. It heats the ground.

Then the ground warms the air above it!

Warm air rises

Sun heats ground

More air rushes in

Ground warms air

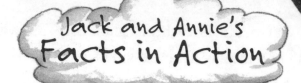

You can see warm air rising if you watch a hot-air balloon take off.

Hot-air balloons fly because the warm air inside is lighter than the cooler air outside! Here's how it works:

1. Burner warms air inside balloon.
2. Warm air inside balloon becomes lighter than air outside.
3. Warm air rises—taking balloon along!

Burner

High Pressure and Low Pressure

Because cold air weighs more than warm air, it *presses* down harder on Earth's surface. So meteorologists call an area of cold air a *high-pressure area*.

Since warm air is lighter, it doesn't press down as hard on Earth's surface as cold air. So meteorologists call an area of warm air a *low-pressure area*.

Air always moves from high-pressure areas to low-pressure areas.

Winds Around the World

The area around the middle of Earth is called the *equator* (ih-KWAY-tur).

The weather is always warmer near the equator than it is at the North Pole or South Pole. That's because Earth is tilted as it travels around the sun.

At the poles, the sun shines down at an angle. At the equator, the sun almost always shines straight down.

Earth

Equator

Sun

Every day, warm air near the equator rises high into the sky. The warm air moves toward the North Pole and South Pole. At the same time, the cold air at the North and South Poles moves toward the equator.

Because Earth is constantly spinning, the moving air doesn't travel in a straight line. It curves and travels around Earth. This traveling air often brings big changes in the weather.

The air we breathe every day has been all around the world!

The Wind at Work

We can't see wind, but we *can* see the wind at work!

Sails push boats across the water.

Wind chimes make music.

30

3

Clouds

Even when you can't see it, there is always water in the air. The invisible water in the air is a gas, like oxygen and carbon dioxide. It is called *water vapor*.

The amount of water vapor in the air is called <u>humidity</u> (hyoo-MID-uh-tee).

The bits of water that make up water vapor are very, very tiny. That's why water vapor is invisible!

Warm air can hold lots of water vapor. But as warm air rises farther and farther from Earth's surface, it begins to cool off.

33

Cool air can't hold nearly as much water vapor as warm air. So as the warm air rises, some of its water vapor starts to *condense*. That means it changes from a gas into tiny droplets of liquid water. If the air is very cold, the droplets may freeze into ice crystals.

The tiny droplets of water and ice crystals make clouds.

When you see your breath on a cold day, you're seeing condensed water vapor!

How Clouds Form

Warm air, full of water vapor, rises

Rising air cools off

Water vapor condenses into water
  droplets and ice crystals

Water droplets and ice crystals
  form clouds

Turn the page to learn about
different kinds of clouds.

Cirrus Clouds

(SIH-rus)

Means "lock of hair" in Latin.

About 7 miles above Earth.

Cirrus clouds are feathery and white. They float very high in the sky. They are made mostly of ice crystals blown by the wind. They usually form when the weather is fair.

Cirrus clouds are sometimes called *mare's tails*. That's because a cirrus cloud can look like the tail of a horse!

Stratus Clouds

(STRAA-tus)

Means "layer" or "cover" in Latin.

About 1 mile above Earth.

Stratus clouds are gray and flat. They often cover the whole sky. They can be made of water droplets or ice crystals.

Some stratus clouds are so low that they hide the tops of hills and buildings. *Fog* is a stratus cloud that touches the ground.

When clouds cover the whole sky, we say the sky is <u>overcast</u>.

37

Cumulus Clouds

(KYOOM-yuh-lus)

Means "heap" in Latin.

About 3 miles above Earth.

Cumulus clouds look like puffs of cotton. They are made up mostly of water droplets. They often appear in the sky during periods of fair weather.

Cumulus clouds are constantly changing shape. It can be fun to find "pictures" in cumulus clouds!

Cumulonimbus Clouds

(KYOOM-yuh-lo-NIM-bus)

Means "heap of rain" in Latin.

About 2–3 miles above Earth.

Cumulonimbus clouds are cumulus clouds that have grown tall and dangerous. They are caused by strong updrafts. These clouds are filled with swirling air, water, and ice. They are where thunderstorms and tornadoes are born.

Cumulonimbus clouds can be over 12 miles from top to bottom!

39

4

Rain and Storms

As the tiny droplets of water in a cloud blow around, they often bump into each other. Some stick together and make bigger drops. The drops keep bumping into each other and get bigger and bigger. As the drops get bigger, they also get heavier.

If the drops get too heavy to be carried by the wind inside the cloud, they fall to the ground. That's rain!

Rain can fall as a gentle shower or a light drizzle. It can also fall as part of a violent storm. If conditions are right, storms can bring lightning, thunder, and hail.

Lightning and Thunder

Inside a storm cloud, the air is very active. Wind is swirling. Water droplets and ice crystals are blown up and down with great force. A storm cloud can look like a huge floating pot of boiling soup!

Storm cloud

All the action inside a storm cloud
can create electricity. The electricity
can cause a giant spark. This spark is
lightning.

Lightning can jump from place to place inside a cloud. It can shoot from one cloud to another. It can also jump from a cloud to the ground. That's when it's *really* dangerous!

Lightning is hot! Meteorologists think a bolt of lightning can be five times as hot as the surface of the sun.

When lightning flashes, the great heat causes the air around the flash to expand very quickly. The expanding air makes a sound like an explosion. That sound is *thunder*.

To **expand** means "to spread out in all directions."

Lightning & Thunder

Giant electric spark

Hot!

Air expands quickly

Makes sound—thunder!

In the United States, thunderstorms happen most often in spring and summer. That's because there's more warm, humid air then to make storm clouds.

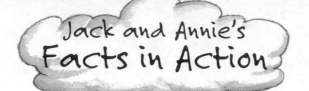

Jack and Annie's
Facts in Action

Thunder can tell you how far away lightning is.

You almost always see lightning before you hear thunder. That's because light travels about a million times faster than sound!

It takes sound about five seconds to travel one mile.

So to figure out how far away a lightning flash is:

1. Count the seconds between the lightning flash and the sound of thunder.

2. Divide by 5.

3. That's how many miles away the lightning is!

Hail

Sometimes the water from a storm cloud falls as chunks of ice. The ice chunks are called *hail*, or *hailstones*.

A hailstone forms when an updraft carries a water droplet high inside a tall cloud. The air near the top of a cloud can be very cold. When the droplet reaches the cold air, it freezes. The droplet then becomes a tiny hailstone.

As the hailstone falls back through the

damp cloud, it gathers a layer of moisture on the outside. The wet hailstone is caught by another updraft. The updraft takes it high into the cloud again. The layer of moisture freezes and the hailstone gets bigger.

This can happen many times. The hailstone gets bigger with every trip up and down inside the cloud. Finally, the hailstone gets too heavy to be lifted by updrafts. When that happens, it falls to the ground.

If you cut open a hailstone, you can see rings. They show how many times the hailstone has been up and down in a cloud!

Hailstones come in all sizes. Some are smaller than blueberries. Others are bigger than softballs.

Hailstones can cause great damage. They can destroy crops, dent cars, and kill small animals. Some have even killed people!

The Coffeyville hailstone

The biggest hailstone ever recorded in the United States fell in Coffeyville, Kansas, in 1970. It weighed nearly two pounds!

The End of a Storm

Most thunderstorms last from 20 minutes to an hour. During that time, warm air rising from the ground keeps feeding the storm with moisture.

Eventually, the rain, hail, and cool air chill the ground. There are no more warm updrafts to feed the clouds. All the water inside the clouds has fallen. The sky clears and the storm is over.

That's what usually happens. But sometimes a thunderstorm can give birth to one of the scariest storms on Earth: a *twister*!

Turn the page for some storm safety tips.

This way

Annie's Storm Safety Tips

You don't need to be afraid of storms. But you do need to know what to do to stay safe if you're caught in one.

Safety tip #1

Go indoors! Your home is probably the safest place for you to be during a storm. Stay away from windows and don't use the phone.

Safety tip #2

Get out of the water! Never swim or take a bath during a thunderstorm. Water carries electricity!

Safety tip #3

If you can't get indoors before a storm hits, stay away from metal fences, pipes, and wires. They can carry electricity from lightning. Also, never ride your bike during a thunderstorm.

Safety tip #4

If you're in a car, don't get out. A car is good protection from rain *and* lightning.

Safety tip #5

Don't take shelter under a tree. Lightning usually strikes the tallest thing around.

5

Twisters!

Twisters, or *tornadoes*, often take people by surprise. They can form very quickly during powerful thunderstorms. Once they hit the ground, they can travel faster than a running racehorse.

Most twisters last only a few minutes. But they leave a path of terrible destruction behind.

Tornado comes from the Latin word **tonare**, which means "thunder."

Tornado Alley

There are tornadoes all over the world. But most tornadoes strike in the mid-western United States. There are so many twisters in this area that it's called "Tornado Alley."

Tornadoes in Tornado Alley usually happen in the spring and early summer. At that time of year, very warm, moist air blows north from the Gulf of Mexico. At the same time, warm, dry air blows east from the Rocky Mountains and cool, dry air blows south from Canada.

Three out of every four tornadoes in the world happen in the United States.

In Tornado Alley, the cool air bumps into the warm air. The meeting causes many violent thunderstorms. Some of these thunderstorms give birth to tornadoes.

Cool, dry air

Canada

Rocky
Mountains

Nebraska

Tornado Alley

Kansas

Missouri

m, dry air

Oklahoma

Texas

Warm moist air

Mexico

During April, May, and June, there are
more than 30 twisters in Tornado
Alley every week!

57

How a Tornado Forms

The thunderstorms most likely to give birth to tornadoes are called *supercells*. Supercells are huge storms. They spread out over 100 square miles. Some last more than three hours. Most have hail, heavy rains, and very strong winds.

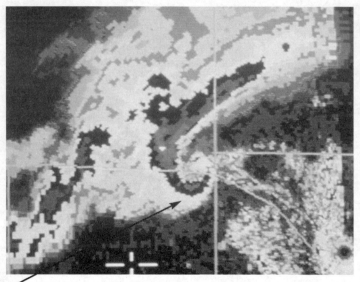

This is a computer picture of a supercell. The hook shape means tornadoes might be about to form.

58

Meteorologists don't know exactly why some supercells create tornadoes and others do not. But they do have a good idea of what happens inside a supercell while a tornado is forming.

1. A strong wind blows over another wind coming from the opposite direction. This causes the air to spin, like a barrel rolling on its side.

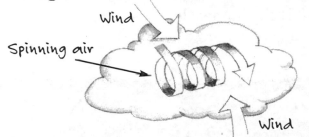

2. An updraft knocks the spinning air on its end. Now it's spinning upright, like a top. When this happens, it's called a *funnel cloud*.

3. Because the storm is spinning, too, the funnel cloud spins faster and faster. It gets longer and longer. Eventually, it pushes down through the bottom of the storm cloud.

4. If the funnel cloud hits the ground, it's a tornado!

Tornado Damage

The winds that swirl in a tornado's funnel cloud can reach 300 miles per hour. That's faster than the fastest race car in the world! Winds from a tornado can easily overturn trucks and destroy homes.

Tornado winds are the fastest winds on Earth.

A tornado in Oklahoma once destroyed a whole motel. People later found the motel's sign in Arkansas!

The funnel cloud of a tornado is like the hose of a gigantic vacuum cleaner. It sucks up everything it touches—dirt, crops, cars, water, animals, people—and drops them farther along its path.

Tornadoes have sucked up whole ponds with everything in them. When the tornadoes dropped the water, people thought it was raining frogs and fish!

Sometimes a tornado seems to "hop" along its path. Such a tornado can tear one house to pieces and leave the house next door untouched.

A tornado moves along the ground at speeds of up to 50 miles per hour. Its path can be up to a mile wide. But the path of most tornadoes is much more narrow.

Twisters are fierce, but they do not last

Jack's Tornado Safety Guide
Here are some tips to keep you safe
 from tornadoes:

1. Know when a twister is coming!

Listen to the radio or TV for tornado watches and warnings in your area.

A tornado *watch* means conditions are right—tornadoes might be coming! Stay tuned for more information!

A tornado *warning* means tornadoes have been spotted! Get ready!

very long. Most are over in just a few minutes.

There is another kind of deadly storm that can last for days, or even weeks. It's called a *hurricane*!

2. Take shelter!

Go to your basement or cellar if you have one. If you don't, go to a closet or bathroom on the first floor of your house (a room without windows is best).

3. Stay inside till the storm is over!

Keep a radio on. Listen for an "all clear" message.

Twister Relatives

Waterspouts

Waterspouts are tornadoes that form over oceans or lakes. Their spinning winds suck up water instead of dirt and dust.

Waterspouts are not nearly as powerful as tornadoes. They rarely have wind speeds over 50 miles per hour. But they can be very dangerous to boats and coastal towns.

Waterspout

Dust devil

Some ancient people thought dust devils were ghosts!

Dust Devils

Dust devils happen mostly in desert areas on hot days. A dust devil sucks sand and dirt into a tall, spinning tube. The tube can be a half mile high!

Dust devils don't usually do much damage. Their wind speeds are less than 50 miles per hour.

67

6

Hurricanes

Hurricanes are the most dangerous storms on Earth. In 1992, a hurricane in Florida destroyed more than 25,000 homes. In 1970, a hurricane in Pakistan killed more than 300,000 people. Every year hurricanes cause billions of dollars worth of property damage around the world.

Why are hurricanes so deadly? The winds of a hurricane are only about half

Hurricane comes from the Spanish word huracán, which means "big wind."

as fast as those of a tornado. But a hurricane can be 2,000 times as wide! And while most tornadoes last less than an hour, hurricanes can rage for many days.

Flooding from
Hurricane Ginger

 In 1971, Hurricane Ginger lasted for over three weeks!

How Hurricanes Form

Hurricanes start over the ocean. They begin as groups of thunderstorms near the equator.

The area near the equator is called the *tropics* (TROP-ix). The climate in the tropics is warmer than anywhere else on earth. The warm temperature means the air in the tropics can hold lots of water vapor.

Climate is the average weather of a place.

A *tropical storm* happens when several thunderstorms join together over an ocean in the tropics. If conditions are right, the storms begin to spin together. If the spinning winds reach 39 miles per hour, it's a tropical storm.

Australians call hurricanes willy-willies.

As the tropical storm drifts across the ocean, it picks up more and more moist ocean air. It spins faster and grows larger.

71

If the winds of the tropical storm reach 74 miles per hour, it's a hurricane!

Hurricane Georges, 1998

The Eye of a Hurricane

The center of a hurricane is the *eye*. In most hurricanes, the weather in the eye is very different from the raging storm around it.

The air in the eye is usually calm. The temperature is warm. The sun shines down from above.

Eye

Spinning winds (at least 74 miles per hour)

In the western Pacific, hurricanes are called typhoons.

When the eye of a hurricane passes over, it might seem that the storm has ended. But once the eye has passed, the storm begins again. That's because the hurricane is just as violent on the other side!

A typhoon in Guam

Hurricane Damage

By the time a hurricane reaches shore, it can be 500 miles wide. Its winds can blow at speeds over 150 miles per hour.

Hurricane winds can blow down office buildings, piers, power lines, and homes. They can rip trees up by the roots. In 1989, Hurricane Hugo completely destroyed several forests in South Carolina.

Hurricane Ginger, 1971

Hurricanes also sometimes give birth to tornadoes, whose winds do even more damage.

Water from a hurricane can also cause terrible destruction. A hurricane can dump several feet of rain in just one day. It can cause ocean waves to swell over 60 feet high!

Hurricane Felix, 1995

Rain from a hurricane can make rivers and streams overflow in areas hundreds of miles away from the center of the storm. The flooding can destroy homes and crops.

Hurricane Floyd, 1999

Storm Surges

The worst hurricane damage is often caused by a *storm surge*. A storm surge is like a giant wall of water pushed onshore by hurricane winds.

Hurricane Eloise, 1975

Hurricane Carol, 1954

The storm surge of a powerful hurricane can cause coastal waters to rise 20 feet above normal. That means every building near the ocean shorter than two stories would be underwater!

Most hurricanes die at sea when they pass over areas of cooler water.

The Death of a Hurricane

Like all storms, a hurricane ends when there is no more warm, moist air to keep it going. Once it begins to travel over land, a hurricane becomes less and less

Naming Hurricanes

Hurricanes have names so meteorologists (and everyone else!) can keep track of them.

Hurricanes get their names when they're still tropical storms. Each year the first tropical storm of the season is given a name beginning with "A." For the rest of the season, the name of each new tropical storm begins with the next letter of the alphabet. If a tropical storm becomes a hurricane, the hurricane keeps the name!

violent. It eventually becomes just another rainstorm. Finally, it dies away completely.

Unfortunately, most hurricanes that hit the shore do serious damage before this happens.

This season's first hurricane is Hurricane Annie!

Until 1979, all hurricanes had girls' names. Now they have boys' names, too!

Andrew: A Historic Hurricane

Hurricane Andrew hit Florida at dawn on August 24, 1992. Andrew raged over Florida for two days, then roared into Louisiana.

Hurricane Andrew caused over $30 billion in damage. It was the costliest natural disaster in the history of the United States.

Fortunately, few lives were lost because the National Hurricane Center warned people that Hurricane Andrew was coming. Nearly 3 million people in Florida, Louisiana, and Texas left their homes and fled to safety.

7

Blizzards

Tornadoes usually strike in spring and summer. Most hurricanes rage in the fall. *Blizzards* are storms that happen in winter.

Winter storms often produce snow instead of rain. That's because in winter, the air inside clouds—and the air below—is much colder.

When water vapor condenses inside very cold clouds, most of it freezes into ice crystals. The ice crystals blow around inside the cloud and stick to each other. When they grow too big and heavy to be carried by the moving air inside the cloud, they fall as snowflakes.

Snowfall can be beautiful and gentle. But when very cold temperatures, strong winds, and heavy snowfall combine, we have blizzards.

In a blizzard, winds over 35 miles per hour blow the snow with great force. Sometimes there's so much blowing snow that you can't see anything at all. This is called a *whiteout*.

6 feet
4 inches

SILVER LAKE

The most snowfall in a single day—over six feet—fell on Silver Lake, Colorado, in 1921.

Blizzards claim fewer lives than hurricanes or tornadoes. But they are still very dangerous. They can knock out the electricity for a whole city. They can strand people in their homes for days or even weeks. They can cause car accidents and plane crashes.

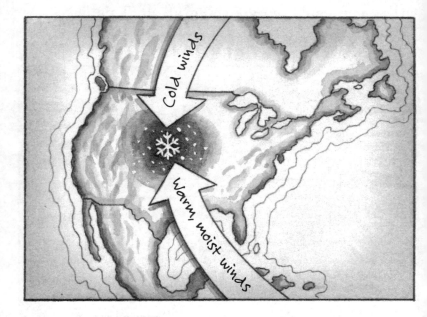

 Most blizzards in the United States happen when warm, moist winds from the Gulf of Mexico bump into cold winds from Canada.

The Blizzard of 1888

One of the worst blizzards in history happened over a hundred years ago in New York City. On March 12, 1888, the people of New York were expecting spring weather to arrive soon. In the late afternoon, a gentle rain began falling. The weather forecast called for a few light snow flurries.

A prediction of weather is called a weather forecast.

The forecast was wrong. The temperature fell during the night. The light rain became heavy snow. The wind picked up.

By the afternoon of the next day, the wind was blowing at 75 miles per hour. It ripped roofs off buildings. It tore down telephone lines. It covered whole houses with snow.

Newspapers reported that people on the street were blown around like dolls.

Many were stranded in their homes or offices.

Hundreds of people died in New York during the blizzard. Hundreds more were killed as the blizzard raged from Maine to Maryland.

People in New York did not know the blizzard was coming. They had no time to prepare. Many deaths might have been prevented if weather forecasts in those days had been more accurate.

Jack and Annie's
Facts in Action

Snow in a blizzard is dangerous. But snow can also be fun!

All snowflakes have six sides . . .

But no two snowflakes are exactly alike!

92

Here's a way you can study snowflakes up close:

Put a piece of black construction paper in the freezer overnight.

Take the paper outside when it's snowing. Catch some flakes on the paper.

Look at the flakes with a magnifying glass. Draw all the shapes you see!

8

Storm Prediction

Meteorologists can't stop tornadoes, hurricanes, or blizzards. But each year they save thousands of lives by letting people know when storms are coming.

Meteorologists have many ways of figuring out what the weather will probably be like from day to day. The secret of predicting the weather is getting *lots* of information.

Weather Watching

There are over 50,000 weather stations around the world. Instruments at the weather stations measure the temperature of the air. They record wind direction and speed. They check for any changes in humidity.

High above the weather stations, special weather planes fly through storm clouds. The planes take pictures. They check air temperature and wind speed. They measure the humidity and air pressure. Some of these planes can fly into the eye of a hurricane!

Weather plane

Weather balloon

Twice a day, meteorologists around the world send weather balloons even higher into the sky. Instruments in the balloons check the weather conditions many miles above the ground.

From space, weather satellites take pictures of Earth. The pictures show where storms are forming. Special kinds of cameras show areas of hot and cold temperatures.

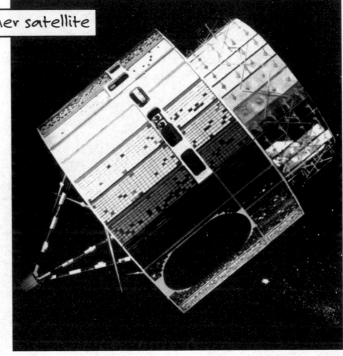

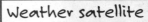
Weather satellite

Satellite pictures can tell meteorologists how fast a hurricane is moving. They can also show where a supercell might create a tornado.

Satellite photo of Hurricane Anita, 1977

Radar dish

Meteorologists also use *radar* (RAY-dar) to help them predict storms. Radar uses radio waves to note tiny changes in humidity and rainfall. Radar can show where the heaviest rain is falling in a hurricane. It can find the storms most likely to produce tornadoes.

Making Predictions

Meteorologists use computers to help turn all this information into weather forecasts. Accurate information helps them predict when and where a storm is likely to hit. If the storm is very severe, people are told to get out of the area. For less severe storms, they're told to take shelter, stock up on food, and prepare for the bad weather to come.

Forecasts are usually updated every six hours. During severe weather, they're updated more often.

101

Meteorologists keep learning better ways to predict the weather. The more they learn, the more lives will be saved.

Storm Chasers

Some people study twisters and other storms up close. These people call themselves "storm chasers."

Storm chasers

Storm chasers learn where a tornado is about to strike. They race to the spot and set up instruments to gather information from *inside* the storm. They take photos and videos. Then they get out of the way before the storm hits!

The information storm chasers gather is useful for helping predict storms. It also helps meteorologists understand how and why storms form. But storm chasing is very dangerous!

If you hear that a storm is about to hit your area, *stay inside!* Listen to the radio or watch television to find out what you should do.

The best way to keep safe is to know when a storm is coming so you can be ready. Remember, storms can be exciting, but they're a *very* dangerous part of our weather!

The Weather at Work

Twisters, hurricanes, and blizzards do lots of damage every year. But storms do a lot of good, too. Thunderstorms cool off a hot day and bring needed water to crops. Heavy rains clean the air. Melting snow from blizzards and other winter storms feeds rivers and streams. Winds blowing around Earth help keep any place from getting too hot or too cold.

Changes in the weather also make life interesting. Imagine what it would be like if the weather were exactly the same every day!

You can have fun being a young meteorologist. Check out the weather where you live. Draw pictures of different kinds of clouds. Measure the rainfall in your own backyard. Make notes of how the weather changes, and how it makes you feel.

Weather is an amazing and wonderful part of our world. Enjoy it!

Doing More Research

There's a lot more you can learn about tornadoes, hurricanes, blizzards, and other kinds of weather. The fun of research is seeing how many different sources you can explore.

Books

Most libraries and bookstores have books about all kinds of storms.

Here are some things to remember when you're using books for research:

1. You don't have to read the whole book. Check the table of contents and the index to find the topics you're interested in.

2. Write down the name of the book.

When you take notes, make sure you write down the name of the book in your notebook so you can find it again.

3. Never copy exactly from a book.

When you learn something new from a book, put it in your own words.

4. Make sure the book is <u>nonfiction</u>.

Some books tell make-believe stories of twisters and other kinds of storms. Make-believe stories are called *fiction*. They're fun to read, but not good for research.

Research books have facts and tell true stories. They are called *nonfiction*. A librarian or teacher can help you make sure the books you use for research are nonfiction.

Here are some good nonfiction books about the weather, and about twisters and other kinds of storms:

- *The Best Book of Weather* by Simon Adams

- *Changing Weather: Storms* by Bobbie Kalman

- *Hurricane and Tornado*, a DK Eyewitness Book, by Jack Challoner

- *Inside Hurricanes* by Mary Kay Carson

- *Tornadoes* by Seymour Simon

- *Twisters!* by Lucille Recht Penner

- *Weather*, a DK Eyewonder Book

Science and Nature Museums

Science and nature museums often have weather exhibits. These exhibits can help you understand more about the science behind twisters and other storms.

When you go to a museum:

1. Be sure to take your notebook!
Write down anything that catches your interest. Draw pictures, too!

2. Ask questions.
There are almost always people at museums who can help you find what you're looking for.

3. Check the calendar.
Many museums have special events and activities just for kids!

Here are some museums around the country with weather exhibits:

- Denver Museum of Nature and Science

- Exploratorium (San Francisco)

- Franklin Institute (Philadelphia)

- Miami Science Museum

- New York Hall of Science

- Science Museum of Minnesota (St. Paul)

- Smithsonian National Air and Space Museum (Washington, D.C.)

DVDs

There are some great nonfiction DVDs about storms and the weather. As with books, make sure the DVDs you watch for research are nonfiction!

Check your library or video store for these and other nonfiction titles about storms and the weather.

- *Forces of Nature*
  from National Geographic

- *Full Force Nature*
  from Echo Bridge Home Entertainment

- *Nature's Fury*
  from National Geographic

The Internet

Many websites have facts about twisters and other storms. Some also have games and activities that can help make learning about weather even more fun.

Ask your teacher or your parents to help you find more websites like these:

- eo.ucar.edu/webweather/

- fema.gov/kids/tornado.htm

- kids.earth.nasa.gov/archive/hurricane/

- www.nssl.noaa.gov/primer/tornado /tor_basics.html

- skydiary.com/kids

- theweatherchannelkids.com/

- weatherwizkids.com /weather-hurricane.htm

- whyfiles.org/013tornado/index.html
- wildwildweather.com/twisters.htm

Good luck!

Index

116

Enough cool facts
to fill a tree house!

Jack and Annie have been all over the world in their adventures in the magic tree house. And they've learned lots of incredible facts along the way. Now they want to share them with you! Get ready for a collection of the weirdest, grossest, funniest, most all-around amazing facts that Jack and Annie have ever encountered. It's the ultimate fact attack!

Have you read the adventure that matches up with this book?

Don't miss

Magic Tree House® #23

TWISTER ON TUESDAY

Jack and Annie are blown away on an adventure when their tree house whisks them back to the 1870s. They land on the prairie near a one-room schoolhouse, where they meet a teenage schoolteacher, some cool kids, and one big, scary bully. But what will they do when the *biggest* and *scariest* thing comes along?

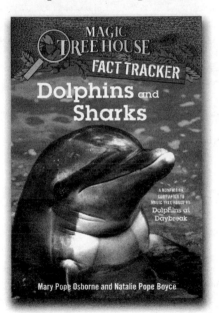

Magic Tree House®

Magic Tree House® Merlin Missions

Magic Tree House®
Super Edition

#1: WORLD AT WAR, 1944

Magic Tree House®
Fact Trackers

DINOSAURS
KNIGHTS AND CASTLES
MUMMIES AND PYRAMIDS
PIRATES
RAIN FORESTS
SPACE
TITANIC
TWISTERS AND OTHER TERRIBLE STORMS
DOLPHINS AND SHARKS
ANCIENT GREECE AND THE OLYMPICS
AMERICAN REVOLUTION
SABERTOOTHS AND THE ICE AGE
PILGRIMS
ANCIENT ROME AND POMPEII
TSUNAMIS AND OTHER NATURAL DISASTERS
POLAR BEARS AND THE ARCTIC
SEA MONSTERS
PENGUINS AND ANTARCTICA
LEONARDO DA VINCI
GHOSTS
LEPRECHAUNS AND IRISH FOLKLORE
RAGS AND RICHES: KIDS IN THE TIME OF
   CHARLES DICKENS
SNAKES AND OTHER REPTILES
DOG HEROES
ABRAHAM LINCOLN

PANDAS AND OTHER ENDANGERED SPECIES
HORSE HEROES
HEROES FOR ALL TIMES
SOCCER
NINJAS AND SAMURAI
CHINA: LAND OF THE EMPEROR'S GREAT
   WALL
SHARKS AND OTHER PREDATORS
VIKINGS
DOGSLEDDING AND EXTREME SPORTS
DRAGONS AND MYTHICAL CREATURES
WORLD WAR II

More Magic Tree House®

GAMES AND PUZZLES FROM THE TREE HOUSE
MAGIC TRICKS FROM THE TREE HOUSE
MY MAGIC TREE HOUSE JOURNAL
MAGIC TREE HOUSE SURVIVAL GUIDE
ANIMAL GAMES AND PUZZLES
MAGIC TREE HOUSE INCREDIBLE FACT BOOK